PRIVATE SOCIAL INVESTMENT TRENDS IN LATIN AMERICA

Chairman of the Board
Celso Varga

President Director
Marcos Kisil

Chairman of the Board of Trustees
Dominic Casserley

Chief Executive
John Low

STATE GOVERNMENT OF SÃO PAULO

Governor
Geraldo Alckmin

CIVIL HOUSE

Chief of staff
Sidney Beraldo

imprensaoficial

President Director
Marcos Antônio Monteiro

PRIVATE SOCIAL INVESTMENT TRENDS IN LATIN AMERICA

Helena Monteiro
Marcos Kisil
Márcia Kalvon Woods

IDIS is a social organization of public interest (OSCIP), founded in 1999 with the objective of promoting the engagement of individuals, families, businesses and communities in strategic social action which are capable of transforming reality, contributing to the reduction of social inequalities in Brazil. Therefore, makes available to social investors innovative and effective ways to invest resources in the social area. Its mission is "Promote and structure private social investment as a tool for the development of a more equitable and sustainable society."

This publication was produced after the event **The Future of Private Social Investment in Latin America Leadership Forum**, held from 23 to 25 September 2007 in Sao Paulo, the objective of which was to provide an environment for reflection, in which the exchange of knowledge and experience would create possibilities to explore the challenges and the role of private social investment (individuals, companies and families) in Latin America for the years to come.

For more information on IDIS, please visit: **www.idis.org.br**

CAF Charities Aid Foundation

The Charities Aid Foundation is a registered charity in the United Kingdom that works to create greater value for charities and social enterprise. We do this by transforming the way donations are made and the way charitable funds are managed.

Our vision
A society motivated to give ever more effectively, transforming lives and communities around the world.

Our mission
An integrated customer-focused organisation for donors and charities that stimulates giving, social investment and the effective use of funds.

Our promise
To be transformational across every aspect of the business.

Our impact
We distribute over £1m to charities on each working day of the year. And through the bank we own, our higher interest rates and lower fees mean an extra £20m goes to the charity sector each year.

Our services
Our core activity is to provide innovative financial services to charities and their supporters:
• for individuals we make it easy to give, to find charities and to support them tax-efficiently
• for companies we set up giving, volunteering and community programmes
• for charities we offer low-cost banking, investment and fundraising
• We work as a CAF International Network with offices in the United States, Australia, Brazil, India, Russia, South Africa, Bulgaria, Singapore and the United Kingdom.

IDIS is responsible for the performance of CAF in Latin America and is part of its international network. The partnership, signed in late 2005, is a decision that is part of CAF's new global strategy. Both organizations agree to act together in the area of private social investment.

To learn more about CAF, visit: **www.cafonline.org**

We acknowledge the support of the sponsors – Fundação Vale do Rio Doce, Banco do Brasil, Gerdau, Instituto Camargo Corrêa, Fundación Loma Negra, which with their support made it possible to hold this meeting. The cooperation of everyone is essential to the dissemination of private investment.

INDEX

Preface 9
Presentation 15
Social Investor in Latin America Profile:
    regional characteristics, global influences 19
Panoramas of private social investment 25
    Global Context: a Changing Scenery 27
        United States 28
        United Kingdom and Europe 31
        Australia and Asia-Pacific 34
    Regional Context: advances for Social Transformation 39
        Mexico 41
        Argentina 45
        Brazil 47
Social Investment in Latin America: looking to the future 55
    Opportunities and challenges 57
    The company and the family as social investors:
        characteristics, challenges and its relationship with civil
        society and the public sector 63
    Conclusion 68
Annexes 71
Annex A: Event Participants 73
Annex B: Speakers and author's mini-biographies 75

PREFACE

Upon completion of the International Seminar on Social Investment in Latin America it had not yet broken out the economic and financial crisis that is plaguing all societies from the middle of the last half of 2008. So I think this preface should examine some of the possible effects of the crisis on philanthropy in the region, and thus be able to contextualize the results of the workshop that are presented here.

In the last decade, along with stabilizing the economy in several countries in the region, we have witnessed a surge of growth and professionalization of the Third Sector. For example, in Brazil it is undeniable that the best economic conditions found in the post-Real Plan made it possible for companies and individuals to begin investing more resources in projects for the welfare of society, creating a virtuous cycle of development. Therefore, now that the financial markets are going goes through an unprecedented global crisis, it is necessary to understand how and with what intensity the crisis is affecting the Third Sector.

We are not talking about a marginal sector or a sector with reduced economic significance. We are talking about a segment which represents in Brazil nothing less than 5% of the Gross Domestic Product (GDP)[1] and is superior to the mineral extraction industry (oil, iron ore, natural gas, coal, etc.) and greater than of 22 Brazilian states, only behind São Paulo, Rio de

---

1   United Nations Volunteers Program (UNV), 2006

Janeiro, Minas Gerais, Rio Grande do Sul and Parana. It is also estimated that the Third sector – voluntary and not-for-profit sector – employs some 1.5 million people or 5.5% of the employees of all organizations formally registered in the country[2].

The first question we should ask is how this crisis affects this development as it will not have the same impact on the world of philanthropy because of its historical and structural character in each country. In the United States, for example, most grants are institutionalized in foundations, which are organizations built from endowment funds, administered generally conservatively in fixed income assets, as there is a commitment to perpetuity. Although with low interest rates, the yield of these assets has dropped dramatically. The known history of how American philanthropy has responded to various economic crises helps to believe that philanthropy is relatively stable.

There are, however, philanthropic organizations in the United States that are not protected, because they work with more aggressive investments. Some of them have had substantial losses in their endowments as evidenced by a recent study of the Foundation Centre conducted with about 1,200 American foundations[3]:

- Approximately 2/3 of these foundations have reduced the number of projects supported and/or the financial size of aid;
- Approximately 40% of the foundations believe they have to use resources from their endowments to honour their commitments, jeopardizing the capability of future support;
- Approximately half of the foundation decided to find ways of acting that do not involve the donation of resources

In addition to the foundations, the new philanthropists are also suffering the effects of the crisis. They are executives or successful entrepreneurs that, at some point decide to implement innovative programs and projects of social organizations in which they are actively engaged, but which, be-

---

2   FASFIL – Fundações Privadas e Associações sem Fins Lucrativos no Brasil – 2005
3   Foundations Address the Impact of the Economic Crisis April 2009. By Steven Lawrence, Senior Director of Research

ing innovative are of higher risk. The new philanthropists are a result of the economic boom of recent years, people who became more aggressive in their actions with direct investment on programs and projects, and not in the creation of endowments. The amount applied may vary depending on the performance of their business. That is, there is no consistency and commitment to perpetuity as an endowment. Thus, resources dwindled with the crisis and, consequently, their philanthropy.

The scarcity of resources from international sources can have an impact for Brazilian organizations. For example, the reduction of international foundations participating in Brazil since the country has risen to an *emerging* status, forming the group known as BRIC (Brazil, Russia, India and China) is well known. With the current crisis we can expect a decrease of resources from other sources. This is the case of resources from European countries like Germany and the Netherlands, where for several decades the "State of Social Welfare" prevailed. In these countries, taxes are high and some of this revenue is redistributed to developing countries through three channels: political parties, unions and churches, in proportion to the representation of each within the population of voters. Some of these organizations send funds for social projects abroad, including Brazil. With the need to help the financial sector and especially to meet their liquidity and credit commitments, these countries must use internal resources that could be made available to assist foreign organizations. To this situation must be added the possibility of a global recession and the consequent reduction of tax revenues, leading to a reduction of resources that could be donated internationally.

In Brazil, as in most philanthropy in Latin America, few organizations have established a strategic way to create an endowment to ensure their longevity and the consistency of programs. Most of the institutes and philanthropic foundations were based on resources allocated annually by the social investor.

An important feature of the sector is that, according to a study by IPEA in Brazil, two thirds of civil society organizations depend for their sustainability on resources that are generated from the sale of products or services. This means that these organizations are part of the economy and therefore are also likely to suffer the impact of the recession and receive smaller donations from individuals who have to make new arrangements on their domestic economy due to inflation or difficulty in retaining their jobs due to the recession.

Another aspect that affects Brazilian civil society organizations is the gradual dependence of certain organizations on donated resources, or other agreements with the public sector; federal, state or municipal. These resources have grown in importance during the current government. Depending on the intensity of the crisis there is a possibility of scarce resources to be used in programs to safeguard the credit system and the financial system liquidity.

In emerging countries like Brazil and Latin America in general, much of the resources available for social projects is linked to the concept of corporate social responsibility. Companies plan their annual budgets in which a budget for philanthropy is stipulated. That is, companies that suffered large losses on derivatives and the devaluation have had their income affected, obviously reduce their funding for social investment. The same will happen if we have a recession. The consequence is that fewer private resources will be available for social activities.

Companies using social action programs as a makeshift measure of brand communication are the first to reduce investments in programs or close them. The crisis is also affecting companies' attitudes towards corporate social responsibility and sustainability. Certified wood, for example, is losing market share because consumers are making buying decisions based on the best price rather than the origin of the wood. A reduction in staff is also happening without due concern for an organisations commitment regarding its policy of corporate social responsibility.

We must now consider how this overall reduction of resources affects organizations. I believe this situation will open an exceptional opportunity for Latin American societies to begin to separate the wheat from the chaff of philanthropy. If there are less resources, greater competence will be needed in terms of efficiency, effectiveness and effective use of available resources. Such an attitude should be sought by both donor groups and social investors, as well as by civil society organizations that depend on these resources.

Data published in early 2006 by The United Nations Volunteers (UNV), also in partnership with The Johns Hopkins Centre for Civil Society Studies, showed a growth of 71% of the non-profit sector in Brazil over seven years (from 1995 to 2002) – from 190 thousand to 326 thousand organizations. I have no doubt now that many of these organizations are in danger of disappearing. This may cause a merger process or partnership between organizations avoiding competition for resources. This could result in a major review of program and financial planning, as well as management, especially with regard to the efficient and effective use of available resources, and growing concerns about the monitoring and evaluation of actions taken. In this sense, the current crisis can help organizations become more professional in their decisions. This requires improvement in its governance, its professionals or volunteers, its administrative processes, as well as transparency in communicating results to different interest groups that are affected by the organization.

We should not expect changes only in the NGOs. The donor, of course, will be more selective and demand more results. With fewer resources, he will require a qualitative improvement and greater impact on the projects financed. In this sense social investors should seek a better definition of their programmatic focus and operational strategies, avoiding fragmentation of resources, which would significantly reduce the impact.

This effort must occur within each organization and there should be a greater emphasis on network performance for a cause, to leverage resources from partners and attract other investors to the cause. Movements such as "Todos pela Educação" -All for Education – , which bring together several organizations to strengthen a single cause will gain importance because this type of efficiency will be increasingly valued.

Thus for a better definition of focus a better understanding of strategic planning should be sought. Especially regarding the definition of what constitutes a strategy for action. These strategies must be based on analytical studies to define the best possible ways to achieve objectives and/or specific goals, applying the best possible means and resources available to make the best use within the context in which the investor intends to work. Instruments for monitoring, control and evaluation must be valued management functions. They should ensure that activities and processes are efficient and effective to achieve the goals of the organization.

Social organizations and social investors who believe that this crisis is only in the financial sector and therefore do not affect their day-to-day may be the first victims. Organizations that realize that they may be affected can take this moment as an opportunity to review their processes and practices. It may provide a good opportunity to prepare for a time when the crises is behind us.

Marcos Kisil

PRESENTATION

The Future of Private Social Investment in Latin America Leadership Forum took place in Sao Paulo, from 23 to 25 September 2007. The event was an initiative of IDIS and the Charities Aid Foundation – CAF. The co-organizers were: the Cemefi – Centro Mexicano para la Philanthropy; GIFE – Group of Institutes, Foundations and Enterprises, from Brazil; and the GDFE – Grupo de Fundaciones y Empresas, from Argentina.

The concept used during the Forum was the same adopted by IDIS: *Private Social Investment is a voluntary and strategic allocation of private resources – whether financial, monetary, human, technical or managerial – for public benefit.*

In this universe of social actions are included businesses, foundations and institutions related to companies or instituted by families or individuals. To make an impact and promote social transformation this investment depends on focused research, creative planning, pre-defined strategies, careful execution and monitoring of results.

The Leaders Forum offered a platform for dynamic debate and an exchange of ideas and experiences. It was attended by leaders from more than 12 countries in Latin America, Europe, Australia and the United States, with vast experience and expertise in private social investment, which offered a rich and valuable contribution to discussions on the regional and global context of private social investment. This document represents an effort to bring to the public the richness of the debate.

INTRODUCTION

LATIN AMERICA SOCIAL INVESTORS: REGIONAL CHARACTERISTICS, GLOBAL INFLUENCES

IDIS experience can contribute to the debate on the issue of social investment. Since its founding in 1999, more than 100 clients in Brazil and Latin America were guided by our Institute. We estimate that these social investors are currently donating around R$500 million per year.

Despite more than 10 years of experience, social investment is still a novelty in Latin America. Our actions are still charitable and caring, trying to correct the effects and not the causes of social problems. In our experience, by contemplating the panorama of social investment we can detect some important challenges for the future of the sector:

1. Lack of transparency, monitoring and evaluation of investment performance: many donors are unaware of the fate of their donation and the results they want to achieve. Even when corporate or family donors create an organization or structure for their donations, they commonly do not act with the necessary professionalism. Many donors have no idea of the impact they could create with their investments;
2. Lack of family tradition: many families do not consider philanthropy as a legacy and inheritance to future generations. Thus, good deeds of one generation are lost in the next generation;
3. Community leaders' lack of knowledge about the potential of local philanthropy: they do not know how the process flows within the community;

4. Lack of focus: the donor does not have a clear focus for his investment and makes sprayed grants, without control;
5. Lack of commitment with reality transformation: donations occur as a mere accounting and finance process. The relationship of the donor with the organization/community ends by the time the resources are transferred.

The data collected on the philanthropist/social investor who acts in our community reveals a lot of information little known about Latin American society. A society with a long history of philanthropy; however, poorly known in its purposes and practices. In this sense, it is still necessary to use information and knowledge generated outside the region to characterize our donors.

Thus, we found an interesting typology, developed by Prince and File to American society, to characterize the different donors. *The Seven Faces of Philanthropy*[4] is a stereotypical way of classifying the behaviour of donors: the devotee, the community, the retributive, the heir, the socialite, the altruistic and the social investor. IDIS experience shows that these types of donors are easily found in every Latin America society, although these types of philanthropists serve to describe the American reality.

The first archetype is the devotee, due to its frequency in a community. He represents those who value religious influence in their lives. Faith leads to the distribution of possessions. They assume the nature of their charitable donations and philanthropy is through religious institutions. He sees the donation as a *tithe* to be paid on a regular basis. Usually participates in the life of his parish, but is not necessarily concerned with the fate of resources. This model, which began in the colonial period, gave rise to charitable organizations in the fields of health (hospitals), education (primary and secondary schools) and social promotion actions (nursing homes, hostels, day care centres). Recently it has become an important instrument of new Pentecostal denominations to build their media structures to act in the society.

---

4 PRINCE, Russ Alan & FILE, Karen Maru. *The seven faces of philanthropy: a new approach to cultivating major donors.*

The second archetype is the Community. In this model the donor believes that his role is important for the improvement of his community. He tries to meet the immediate needs and has difficulty in distinguishing causes and effects. He believes that his solidarity can be easily recognized by their fellow citizens, which strengthens his image, and eventually is good for him socially, politically or purely commercially. Often these donors are also recipients of their own resources as they tend to support social organizations to which they are linked. They usually operate within a closed system and of little transparency. They do not use any strategy to donate.

The third archetype is the retributive. He gives as devolution, that is, as he once was the recipient of help through organisations, now he returns it through the donation. There are donors who have been supported through difficult times in their lives by an organization, whether secular or of religious character, and having succeeded in overcoming them, believe they have a personal debt to be settled by donation.

The fourth archetype is the heir. Although there is still some difficulty in understanding the passage of the philanthropic commitment from one generation to another, there are those who believe there is a family tradition that adds philanthropic work to the inheritance. It is common to see families who run civil society organizations providing services that meet different causes and beneficiaries such as children, elderly, and disabled, among others. The organization becomes an organization that the family has an obligation to support. This passes from generation to generation and the heir continues to maintain that organization through donations.

The fifth pattern is the socialite. The person who promotes charitable events, which are in reality big parties. He donates because it feels pleasant. At the same time as raising funds, he is also having fun. They are usually people who work in exclusive social circles, among friends, and the party is important because it is a way to mobilize resources to be channelled to major social issues. This type of donor does not work for the organization that is supported; he is exclusively dedicated to fundraising.

The sixth archetype is the altruistic. He feels good when he is doing good to others. The altruistic donor believes and is involved with the cause that he is supporting. He is usually modest and prefers to remain anonymous. He gives because he believes in a moral obligation, an intrinsic value which he needs to express. This type of donor is not active in the organizations he supports, because in most cases he is more concerned with social causes: environmental, children, etc. than with the organizations in which his resources are used.

The last archetype is the social investor. It is the individual who IDIS believes and would like to see multiplied in future years as, for him, doing good is in fact a good deal. These are people who already have management experience in their own business and that look to social causes with concern for its impact. They see social investment as a business and really want with their resources to innovate and transform society. They play the role of an active donor, calibrating their donations on the degree of participation that they can have in inspiring, participate in and monitor their investment. They are concerned with the strategic planning, the management, the evaluation of results and the professionalism that occurs in their actions; that is the reason they surround themselves with people who understand the subject.

They do not act alone, they seek partnerships. They have learnt to work with suppliers, with customers, with unions, and they bring this idea to build a network of sustainability for the project. They do not see the sustainability of the resource that they bring, but in the ability to make more people who donate interested in the project by creating ideal conditions of operation after the end of their resources. The profile of this kind of investor is what stands out: young, public people and who have a resume that includes volunteering and philanthropy. People like Sergei Brin, Larry Page, Bill Gates.

According to Forbes magazine, there are 946 billionaires in the world with 3.5 trillion dollars in consolidated assets. What is surprising, however, is that out off the Forbes list of the hundred richest people in the world, 33 billionaires are from countries outside North America and Western Europe; and 17 of them are less than 50 years old. Today there are 14 billionaires in Russia, eight in India, seven in the Middle East, three in Hong Kong and one in Latin America.

It is in this context that the concept of Philanthropy 4.0 emerged, created by the Russian Olga Alexeeva, director of CAF Global Trustees. She proposes an understanding of the philanthropy evolution similar to the understanding of the software programs evolution that is presented progressively in new versions. Philanthropy 4.0 is the evolution of traditional philanthropy. Thus, the Philanthropy 1.0 is the traditional that began with W. K. Kellogg and John D. Rockefeller in the early twentieth century. It was mostly aimed at the creation of libraries, hospitals, and some programs that were designed to create infrastructure that did not exist in the country. Then Philanthropy 2.0 came, when those foundations established significant endowments and funding programs not only in the United States, but in many parts of the world to financially support the world's social change. Philanthropy 3.0 was characterized by new ideas and the greater involvement of donors and foundations in the supported projects.

Philanthropy 4.0 features a philanthropy that has a global scope and face. It is present in developing countries in Asia, Eastern Europe, South America, which have always been seen as recipient countries for donations. In this new model local entrepreneurs and philanthropists work together, joining results and ideas to achieve social transformation. Therefore, it is a more sustainable philanthropy – not just financially, as the social sector is less dependent on international contributions – but also for being more sensitive to local culture, with its identity and the country's history. It is no longer about simply copying the procedures of the West, but considering local culture and respecting it.

In this new philanthropy, the new donors understand their action as social investment, not as charity. They are results oriented, like to take an active role in their donations and, in general, want to apply their business skills to philanthropy. New donors in Russia, China, India and Brazil, besides, of course, those in the United States and Europe fall into this definition.

These new investors generally prefer to design and implement their own ideas and to establish institutions in life instead of grant making foundations to perpetuate their names. They are often younger than traditional philanthropists who made their first social investment at their 60's or 70's. Today, these investors are in their 35's – 45's. In Russia, according to Olga Alexeeva, 80% of billionaires are under 45 years. In China, more than 50% of billionaires are under 45 years. It's worth remembering that Bill Gates made his first billion at 31!

This new philanthropy is younger and less related to retirement and inheritance plans. Considering the lack of tax incentives on most new philanthropic countries – such as Latin America, Russia and China – we see that the growth of new philanthropy is not directly encouraged by legal or tax benefits.

An important point for discussion is foundations. We do not find in Brazil (and it seems in Latin America in general or in Russia and China) that common tradition in the United States to create foundations with endowments. Most foundations in Latin America are operative, rather than donor. That is, they apply part of their resources for the implementation of social programs and projects rather than giving to others. Furthermore, wealth managers and investment professionals are not prepared to work for the social action of investment, they can only see the capacity of profit that comes from money and not the possibility of applying it to social outcomes. Wealth management does not incorporate the idea of social or socio-environmental.

This is the reality in which we find opportunities and challenges that IDIS believes can and should be overcome. This is the reality we want to build for social investment, to be an important element in the sustainable development of our societies. We seek to make social investment fair, innovative, strategic, and reality transforming.

Billionaires, when donors, can be incorporated into a typology that takes into account their motivations. Normally we find three main motivations: the first is conviction. It is the individual who takes the decision to donate because of his values, because he believes in changing the world and has the ability to make his money important. Unfortunately the group of people with that profile is still restricted within the present global scenario.

The second group donates for convenience, it is important because he gets a kind of prestige to the business or for himself. And he is moved by results that can not be acquired by donation, but by his social activity. This type of donor also uses current affairs, detecting what is in fashion and investing in this issue.

The last group consists of individuals who suffer from coercion, not willingly, but compelled by some circumstance; it might be a pressure of context, customers, competitors, employees, community and society or of his friends. He needs to respond to an external force.

Regardless of the source that triggers the desire to make a social investment, our great challenge is to transform any motivation into a permanent commitment. Conviction, coercion and convenience are only the starting points. It is important because we can eventually create different strategies to help specific groups. Our vision is that everyone can develop a continued commitment to social transformation.

PANORAMA OF SOCIAL INVESTMENT

GLOBAL CONTEXT: A CHANGING SCENE

Social private investment in industrialized countries, as in the case of the United States, Australia and the United Kingdom is in full expansion and changing phase. The social investor of today has a new profile; shows little interest in the traditional donation of resources and gives priority to initiatives that enable their engagement and have a focus on results. At this time of transition and innovation it is possible to identify some trends and challenges.

It stands out as a global trend the emergence of new types of social investment; many are hybrid approaches that blend practices of the social and private sectors, such as, social entrepreneurship and venture philanthropy. Therefore, the distinction between business and voluntary sectors becomes increasingly less clear. Nowadays, not only social return is important, but also the economic return of the social investment. This represents a big change, both for social investors, who have traditionally sought social returns, and for the private sector, which has traditionally only focused on the financial return.

This trend brings with it a challenge to be overcome. It is the need to define what belongs to the field of social investment. None of the countries mentioned above have a single, clear definition of social investment which encompasses all its components and models. Between the more traditional models of philanthropy and the most innovative models of social investment, we must define how each will be understood and what is the role played by each in the area of social development.

Another global trend is the desire to reach large-scale results in a short term span. Many of the current social investors built their own fortune dynamically and daringly and want to see this same agility and courage in their social investments. That is, the current scenario is composed of social investors who are entrepreneurs, who generated their own wealth, and who want to see the results of their social investment while they are alive.

The current global context is also a time of significant transfer of wealth between generations, which creates the expectation of a large increase in the volume of private social investment. Today, many of the wealthy people are getting closer to an end in the phase of generating wealth and are beginning to decide how to transfer or distribute their wealth. This has caused a lot of expectation that billionaires will decide, while still alive, to engage in private social investment and that much of this wealth is directed to the social sector.

Finally, this scenario of change and innovation has contributed to greater professionalism, transparency and efficiency of the voluntary and non profit sector. There is a steady increased demand for higher education courses, the production of knowledge and opportunities to exchange experiences among different countries and regions. All this is contributing to the development of a diversified, vibrant and dynamic social sector.

UNITED STATES[5]
Rob Buchanan, International Programmes Director,
Council on Foundations[6]

In the United States there is no single definition that encompasses all components of private social investment. This refers mainly to strategic philanthropy, characterized by having clear objectives, a plan to achieve these goals and a broad concept of social transformation that goes beyond

---

5   Text extracted from the Leadership Forum transcripts: The future of Private Social Investment in Brazil
6   The Council of Foundations is an organisation placed in Washington, DC, USA, which holds about 2100 different members from private family foundations, businesses, corporate foundations and community foundations.

the specific social problems. However, the term private social investment is also used to refer to traditional donations made for social purposes, which is quite popular in the United States; as well as to corporate social responsibility, and to the commercial approach or business models applied to the non-profit sector.

Despite the difficulty of finding a precise definition of private social investment, which encompasses all its aspects, Blended Value[7], offers an interesting definition. According to this organization, private social investment includes investments that seek financial and social return, and can be divided into socially responsible investment, investments that are aligned to the values and business of the company; and other forms of investments in which the main objective is to generate social and/or environmental value.

To understand the role of private social investment in the United States it is important to remember that this country has always had a clear distinction between the private and the non-profit sector. However, since the late 80's, this distinction has been gradually softening, for a number of factors.

One is the difficulty of governmental programs to solve social problems. In the '60s and '70s, the government funded broad social programs, aiming to reduce social problems that affected the country. However, in the late 80's, it was noticed that these programs had failed because they had not tackled the roots of the problems.

In the mid-90's the pension system reform was approved, which led to the renewal of funding policies aimed at the poorest population and the reduction of public funding for social programs. This was a sign of change, a clear message that the reduction in social investment from the government would mean the voluntary and not-for-profit sector taking over part of this role of contributing with the transformation of social reality. As a result, increases the voluntary sector's role and responsibility of dealing with social and environmental issues in the country. It also increases the professionalism of this sector, as civil society organizations had to develop new strategies for sustainability.

---

7   A Blended Value é uma entidade norte-americana que analisa o setor comercial e o setor social sem fins lucrativos tentando criar definições < http://www.blendedvalue.org/>

At the same time, in the 80's and 90's, the expansion of the movement of corporate social responsibility – CSR. There is a new generation of CEOs who were involved in the social unrest movements of the '60s and '70s in the United States and who they feel pressured to address the social agenda. In doing so, they can generate not only social and/or environmental results, but also improvements in the financial performance of these companies.

Finally, we have the great success of IT companies in California which has produced the accumulation of wealth and has spread the concept that private resources, arising from economic activities, can be used to promote social change through innovative approaches. All these factors have contributed to a less clear distinction between the business and voluntary sector.

Nowadays what bridges the boundary between these two worlds is private social investment, through a series of actions that mix business and social intervention models. Therefore, there is today in the U.S. a much less clear distinction between the business and the non-profit sectors, and both business community and social organizations feel the need to continue working in this area to succeed in the model.

The current trend of investing huge amounts of private resources in the social sector raises a new debate. The United States is experiencing a transfer of trillions and trillions of dollars from the generation born right after World War II for their children. There is an expectation that the bulk of these resources should be invested in innovative philanthropic initiatives, as in the United States, unlike in Latin America, individual and family investors have a greater attraction for experimental models and are more willing to take risks. They are more open to risk as they invest their own wealth and their own capital and, as well because many have an entrepreneurial set of mind and want to see results achieved while they still alive. However, there is a growing concern in maximizing the return on social investments.

The increase in the volume of resources invested and the ease of communication offered by the Internet will contribute to greater transparency and accountability across the voluntary sector. For example, the Internet and bloggers can simply disclose to the public what is not working. This year, a problem with the Bill & Melinda Gates Foundation was displayed to the public. It made large investments in areas that went against the social goals of the Foundation. And it was the internet and some blogs that made it public.

We are living in a very interesting time for the sector. Private social investment is in the process of expansion and transition, and there is a lot of innovation focused on the common good.

UNITED KINGDOM AND EUROPE
Russell Prior, executive-director of corporate programs,
CAF International Network

As in the U.S., in Europe there is also the difficulty of establishing a clear definition of social investment. However, the definition that best reflects the current moment of social investment in Europe and the United Kingdom is the one from the *European Venture Philanthropy Association (EVPA)*, which defines social investment as a private equity and venture capital model applied to philanthropic and non-profit sectors. On one hand, financing techniques combining resources, skills and practices; on the other hand, donors who want to maximize social return of their investments. This definition brings new elements, such as venture capital, and different models of financing because in Europe social investment is increasingly moving away from traditional forms of philanthropy.

Europe is a community with many countries and diversity. There is some tension between the Anglo-Saxon model, which is more entrepreneurial and innovative, and the model of continental Europe, which is closer to the traditional format of philanthropy. We can clearly see that in the U.K. philanthropy and social investment have grown strongly since the early '90s. This country is in the vanguard of European social investment, and London, as an important financial centre, is where more innovation is seen.

Eastern Europe, in which many countries have recently joined the European community, the approach is a little less developed, but new approaches are being adopted very quickly. Therefore, the United Kingdom may have taken 15 years to achieve; they will take much less time because they already have the correct tax regulatory framework for the development of philanthropy and social investment. The creation of fiscal environments increasingly favourable to the encouragement of donations has also contributed to the increase in social investment in these countries. At the same time, to the extent that the governments become more democratic, it is also observed a rapid growth of organizations with social purpose.

In Europe, models of social investment are polarized between the more traditional models of philanthropy and more commercial and financial investment patterns. Between these two extremes, there are many models being created, from organizations that sell goods and services for fundraising, through social focused companies that offer social services, to funds that pay part of their profits to non-profit foundations regarding operations show good results.

Currently, social investors expect projects to show transparency and short-term results. This is one of the reasons why so many innovating initiatives are emerging. This search for results is because many of these investors have built their fortune dynamically and want the same in their social investments.

In the same way there was a change in the expectations and attitudes of individual investors, the form in which the government makes its investments in the social sector has also changed. It is observed that public funding is contingent on the provision of services. Thus, the government values the role played by the social sector, but expects the industry to operate more commercially. This change in the government's attitude caused a pressure for results in civil society organizations.

The diagram below shows the degree of correlation between the involvement of donors and the desired return. It shows only some of the many organizations in the United Kingdom operating in this field. There is a tendency for all types of organizations to approach the centre, seeking to place the same importance to social and financial return. This is a big change, both for traditional funds and foundations, whose history demonstrates the importance placed in social return; as well as for banks, which usually sought financial return.

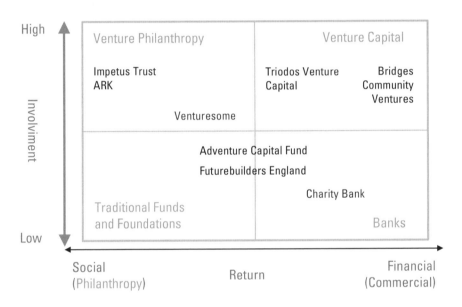

Venturesome, an initiative of CAF, was founded five years ago as a hedge fund to exploit innovations in this market. The idea was to find a space between the donation and loan. It would not be a standard loan from a bank, but would not be a traditional gift, in which there is no expectation of return. They were trying to take more risks and, at the same time, obtain more significant social returns. This would be the balance.

After five years in operation, the Venturesome has already signed hundreds of agreements, has got seven million pounds open, in terms of funding, donation and loan. The expectation of success is 70% of the funds offered. It is an initiative philosophy, as a bank would never accept lead to losses of 30% of the amount invested. Experience has shown that rates of return are close to 90%. Interest rates are not adjusted depending on the risk of proposal because, if so, they would be very high. They are used to charge a rate between 6% and 8%, based on rates available in the UK.

Although **Venturesome** is a fund of seven million pounds, this amount is relatively small in view of the availability of resources for these purposes. However, access to these resources is not easy. So, can this model be applied in emerging economies and markets? Faced with the context and trends of social investment in Europe, some factors may influence the future of social investment in Latin America.

Globalization is constantly changing the way in which the business sector assumes its role in supporting social causes. The combination of the wealth of family foundations, individuals and companies seem to be available to support the sector.

The role played by capital markets can be very important in the future of social investment because companies have knowledge, experience and skills to share. There are many financing models of the social sector emerging from capital market and this expertise is very important in creating these experimental models.

To take advantage of these opportunities, the industry needs to further professionalize and organizations need to be more willing to take risks, to innovate and experiment with new forms of financing. If they are not prepared, capital providers will not have where to invest.

AUSTRALIA AND ASIA-PACIFIC
Michael Liffman, Director, Asia-Pacific Philathropy and Social Investment Centre, Swinburne University

It is very difficult to trace the current context of philanthropy and social investment in the Asia-Pacific region due to its historical and cultural diversity. In some countries, resources from international funding for natural disasters and resources received from expatriates make philanthropy very different in these countries from the one practiced in the West.

Australia, specifically, is experiencing a period of transition because, despite having a strong cultural and institutional British heritage with regard to models of philanthropy and social investment, it is now adopting practices and models that are closer to those in the United States. This is due to the transfer of wealth between generations, a phenomenon that affects the current context of philanthropy and social investment both in the United States and Australia.

The Asia-Pacific region presents certain contradictions in its practice of philanthropy and social investment. On the one hand the region exports models and trends, as the *1% Club*, where the Federation of Korean Industries brings together companies that direct one percent of their gross revenue to social investment; and the *Philippines Business for Social Progress*, which promotes social investment from companies. On the other hand it lacks infrastructure for the development of philanthropy and social investment. In many countries, the media is insensitive to these issues, lack a legal and taxation commitment to promote the development of philanthropy and social investment, and lack experience and knowledge about fundraising and social sector management. Moreover, there are relatively few experiences of alliances and partnerships between government and civil society organizations.

Social investment has been seen as a way to mitigate both the excesses and inequalities of capitalism and the failure of socialism. The actions in this field range from the most traditional forms of charity to the construction of venture capital for social development. The differences between social investment and philanthropy, making appropriate distinctions between welfare, philanthropy and social investment are very important. However, only few organizations in the region have been discussing the issue. *Social Venture Australia* is one of these organizations which is evolving from a more traditional approach to philanthropy to the adoption and promotion of more complex models of social investment.

In these discussions, we must also define how the evolution of a more traditional model of philanthropy to modern models will take place in the light of what we see in the European continent, especially in the United Kingdom. The main objective of social investment is to support results and not intentions. Thus, social investment can be defined as the use of private resources, from companies, families or institutions to achieve results, going beyond intentions. In other words, it supports the attainment of social dividends.

There are two major challenges to be overcome by the Asia-Pacific region to the development of social investment. The first is the lack of professional training opportunities in these areas in the higher education level, unlike the United States, where there are a number of schools that offer training in these areas. Like the corporate world, the world of social investment also seeks return, with the distinction that the return sought is social, as it will transform social reality. Obtaining this kind of return is very complex. While executives of the corporate world receive special training to perform their functions, the same is not true for professionals working in the non-profit sector. Philanthropy and social investment are subjects that should be mandatory in business administration courses. Improvement in training would help with the professionalization of the sector.

The second challenge to be overcome also applies to the North American and European context. Among the traditional models of philanthropy and the newer models there are a number of other models. Among them all, we must define which one really takes part of social investment as more companies will act in the social sector, for various reasons, whether for new opportunities, by privatization, outsourcing of the public to the private sector or other reasons.

In Australia, there have always been homes for the elderly managed by the business sector, doctors and other professionals providing services for social purposes, but they do so for profit. So, it is need of a review of the social investment definition if it should only be applied to civil society organizations, excluding for-profit companies that provide services and develop products for social purposes, occupying positions traditionally filled by the voluntary sector.

Finally, you must change the paradigm that the work of the non-profit is positive and that the work of the sector for profit is negative. There is a case that clearly illustrates the need to change this paradigm. Some years ago, a director of a non-profit organization had the opportunity to make a presentation on the non-profit sector to a great Australian entrepreneur and businessman. On this occasion, the director presented the importance of the non-profit sector. The entrepreneur, in turn, listened to it politely, but at the end of the presentation he thanked him and said he had not understood anything. The businessman gave two reasons for the misunderstanding. First, the presenter spoke of a sector which the businessman little understood of as he operates his business under the logic of profit. For him, it is difficult to understand how organizations survive if not profitable. The voluntary and non-profit sector seeks and should obtain profit. However, this profit is invested in a different way and ensures the sustainability of organizations. So to say that the organization is non-profit may sound misleading.

Then the businessman said: "After your comments, I understand that what I develop in my industrial complex to promote the improvement of living conditions in society (generating thousands of jobs and drive the economy) is not virtuous!" He did not like that perception since the creation of jobs and economic activity by itself can generate social development. In addition, there are many companies making social investment in an innovative way, thinking of reciprocity, using performance indicators and really trying to promote social change.

Among all models of philanthropy and social investment, from the most traditional to the most modern, we must define how each will be understood and what the role it will play in the field of social development.

REGIONAL CONTEXT:
ADVANCES FOR SOCIAL TRANSFORMATION

Over the past 20 years, Latin America has experienced a moment of great conceptual redefinition, involving mainly the concept of citizenship and the non-governmental public sphere. There is a new understanding of the roles that the state, market and civil society play. It is observed in several countries that have a consolidating democracy and hence the rapid creation and development of civil society.

This new scenario has contributed to the strengthening of private social investment in the region, both in terms of awareness of the role of social investor and of the volume of resources invested. It also contributes to the professionalization of the voluntary and non-profit sector, especially in regard to leadership training and management practices.

Despite the great advances of the past 10 years, this new era of private social investment in Latin America still faces many challenges. Unlike the U.S. it still prevails in the region of corporate social investment, with many powerful families choosing to conduct their philanthropy through their company, instead of structuring a family foundation. Although there are many and good experiences of corporate social investment in the region, efforts are also needed to promote family and community social investment models. This diversity of models is necessary for the development of a healthy and robust field of social investment in the region.

In Latin America there is still a charity culture of social investments, which hinders the development of the strategic vision, of addressing the cause of problems and achieving long term sustainable results. The charity approach also makes it difficult for large scale interventions, with the potential to achieve greater impact.

Another major challenge is to communicate the results achieved to society and the government. The current context of social investment in Latin America will greatly benefit from a wider publication of the knowledge gathered in the last 10 years and of a good communication strategy to disseminate it. There is still mistrust on part of the society in regard to private social investment, and much of this distrust is due to a lack of knowledge. For example, there is the erroneous notion that company institutions are only for the company to benefit from tax incentives. However, studies show that it is exactly the opposite, the amount of social investment increases with the creation of an institute, surpassing the amount from tax incentives.

In some countries there is also distrust within society in regard to the reputation and integrity of non-profit organizations. Therefore, we must disseminate good practice, the achievements and value the contribution of businesses, families and communities in social development. Private social investment does not occur in a vacuum, it occurs in a context where there are other actors of equal influence and relevance. Thus it is very important to be aware of its role in the relationship with the government and civil society.

This new era of social investment in Latin America is a consequence of a change in the way the market does business, of the concept of state and of the role of civil society. This requires new attitudes for the social investor. Risk and innovation are some of them. Non-profit organizations should take this opportunity to strengthen and professionalize their work thus; when the social investor is ready to invest it will not be difficult to locate partner organizations. Governments should recognize and support the social investor, through tax policies and other measures to encourage increased donations. In order to scale up and ensure the sustainability of results it is essential that the three sectors work together, adopting practices of collaboration to social development.

MÉXICO
Jorge Villallobos,
Executive President, CEMEFI (Mexican Centre for Philanthropy)

Over the past twenty years Latin America has been undergoing a major conceptual redefinition, involving the concepts of democracy and citizenship. There is a new understanding of the role that the state, civil society and the private sector play in relation to society.

Besides conceptual progress, the region also experienced an amazing economic growth. Three Latin American countries – Brazil, Mexico and Argentina – are now among the 20 largest economies in the world. However, despite the financial success, the challenge of reversing the trend of poverty still remains. This is the great paradox of the region: economical growth but unequal distribution of the wealth.

There is no strong tradition of philanthropy in Latin America. According to the comparative study of the non-profit sector, carried out by Salamon, from Johns Hopkins University (1998) in the 34 countries studied, the donations represent an average of 0.38% of GDP. However, the Latin American average is 0.23%. With respect to funding sources, there are three sources: a) the government, making their contributions of funds through tax exemptions or direct transfers; b) private and corporate philanthropy; and c) the extent of services that are distributed to the organizations of civil society. The average of government transfer to the private sector in public services is 34%, of philanthropy is 12%, and the quotas and services, 53%. In other words, in Latin America, the government contributes very little and philanthropy contributes even less. The major contribution comes from citizens who pay for services, quotas and governmental taxes.

PRIVATE SOCIAL INVESTMENT (VOLUNTEERING AND DONATIONS) IN TERMS OF GDP

Country	Donations (foundations, companies, individuals)	Volunteering	Total
United Kingdom	0.62%	1.96%	2.57%
United States	1.01 %	1.48%	2.47%
Spain	0.87 %	1.25%	2.10%
Argentina	0.38 %	1.03%	1.41%
Colombia	0.32 %	0.28%	0.60%
Peru	0.26 %	0.06%	0.33%
Brazil	0.17 %	0.10%	0.27%
Mexico	0.04%	0.08%	0.12%
Average of the 34 countries	0.388%	1.12%	1.50%
Average LA	0.23	0.31	0.54

Source: Johns Hopkins University, Third Sector Comparative Project 1998

After all, there is a real need to increase philanthropic contributions in the region and better exploit private social investment potential to contribute to social transformation.

In Mexico, there are few studies that provide data on private social investment, and government information is inaccurate. We can however say that the number of donors, particularly foundations and business programs has grown.

Up to 10 years ago, there were no major foundations in Mexico. At the time, the largest was the Mary Street Jenkins Foundation, promoted by an American living in Mexico. Today, this Foundation is the seventh largest in the country because in recent years other large foundations have been created. The Gonzalo Rio Arronte Foundation, created by a Mexican businessman who bequeathed $600 million is now one of the largest in Mexico.

This has set a precedent in the country for the creation of new large foundation such as Carlos Slim Foundation, the Carson Foundation and the Telmex Foundation also operate programs with assets of more than one billion dollars. Another interesting example is the Mexican Fund for Nature Conservation, which was created with a $10 million donation made by the American government with a counterpart from the Mexican government; it was $20 million that passed into private hands to set up the fund. With sound financial management and more donations they were able, after 15 years, to reach the current equivalent of 100 million dollars.

There is also the Nacional Monte de Piedad Foundation, founded in 1775, which give annually around 20 million dollars. Magdalena Brockmann Foundation, Fundación del Empresariado Chihuahuense, Compartir Foundation and the Merced Foundation, and so on.

These are the signs of the new era of philanthropy in Mexico. Historically, the first period of the Mexican Philanthropy, called the colonial, was from 1521 to 1860. This period is characterized by the strong presence of the Catholic Church in the field of social welfare. Education, health, hospitals and care with indigent widows, were responsibilities of the church. The church also owned most of the country and produced the money that was spent socially.

In 1860 there was a reform promoted by President Benito Juarez. Church property was confiscated by the state, which then assumed responsibility for social welfare. This was a very important change for social transformation: what was done in the private sector for religious reasons was now done by the state as its legal obligation.

The second period of Mexican philanthropy goes from 1861 to 1960, when the State takes control of the welfare and creates organizations for this purpose: *"la junta de assistencia privada"*, a control body that prevented the properties to pass into the hands of the church again. With the Mexican Revolution there was a consolidation of the Estate and the establishment of major assistance programs for education, health, housing, etc.

The third period goes from 1961 to 1985, and can be characterized by the emergence of the idea of citizenship. The banner year was 1985, when the country was ravaged by a terrible earthquake. This disaster caused the reaction of civil society, which eventually resulted in the awareness of citizens on social participation, new social causes and the voluntary sector.

The fourth period, beginning in 1986, is marked by the introduction of the concept of philanthropy and volunteerism, promotion of corporate social responsibility, the emergence of new foundations and greater participation in the social sector. In 2004 a new law on tax reform was approved, and was introduced in 2007. Today we live a period of expansion and strengthening of social investment.

During these periods, Mexican philanthropy maintained strong characteristics of welfare that, in a sense, are also present in other Latin American countries. The tradition of social assistance for humanitarian reasons linked to religious motivations – the religious salvation – is very strong in the culture of the region.

There are still challenges for the growth of philanthropy and social investment. The trend of charity is expressed at various levels. Grants are concentrated mainly in welfare programs or additional resources for education and health. Mexican companies give to the government, instead of donating to civil society to strengthen citizenship. The media encourages charitable donations. Even though governments say they want citizens' participation, they have difficulty in giving up their control and still feel uncomfortable with civil society organization. In the legal aspect the logic of welfare means that there is no need for tax benefits as the philanthropist helps because he wants to be a good person.

Still, we live a time of great growth in the number of donors, the amount of donations and the debate over the fate of donations. There is greater awareness among companies, civil society and some government authorities, of the need for private money to complement in actions that can not be done by the government alone.

Finally, private social investment of corporation or individuals continues to be an opportunity to join talent and efforts to contribute to a better and more equitable society in our continent.

ARGENTINA

Carolina Langan,
General Coordinator, Argentina's Group of Fundations and Companies

In Argentina, the great challenge in terms of private social investment lies in innovation and the breadth of its scope to embrace non traditional social causes. In Latin America we have the traditional areas of support such as health, education and community development. The social investor feels comfortable with these areas. A survey of corporate social responsibility in Argentina shows that 88% of respondents are satisfied or highly satisfied with the results of their social interventions. The challenge then is to go beyond compliance. Of course, when good things happen no one wants to change, but we encourage donors to go further to generate transforming programs.

There is also a challenge in terms of support for the so-called "organizations specialized in advocacy actions," since, in general, investors tend to support organizations that offer social services, which is consistent with the high levels of poverty and indigence and the poor networks of public welfare in the region. But it is also important to support organizations that work with specific social causes.

Another interesting challenge is to develop a process that creates in the citizens values of social responsibility, social awareness, under the logic of universal social rights. With this, I refer not only to understand that we all as citizens have rights to certain services, but above all we are entitled to the opportunity to properly appropriate from these goods and services.

It is also important to have access to theoretical knowledge that offers information for choosing a particular strategy or position with respect to the problem. We often focus on the effects of a problem because we do not understand the magnitude, origins and root cause of a particular social problem.

We also need to operate based on diagnosis, which is difficult because often data is non existent, and there is little information available. Thus, the demand for research becomes high. Another challenge concerns the development of technologies, of social engineering. We must learn how to manage our knowledge and how to qualify our learning, so they can be disseminated.

It is the voluntary sector's role to motivate, promote and develop new social investors. In Argentina it is very important to develop private donors, and an actor who is increasingly important is the small and medium enterprises. Moreover, it is the public sector's role to stimulate civil society organizations and private donors, improving tax incentives legislation.

A very interesting topic to be mentioned is that none of the countries of the region is free from disaster or emergency situations. However, we have very little knowledge about the subject. It is important to examine the experiences that other countries have had and learn to act in coordination. I do not know, really, if there was in Argentina today a situation of disaster, emergency, if donors could donate appropriately in an organized way.

In the specific case of Argentina, one of the main challenges is to democratize and federalize the country's social investments. Another major challenge is to have greater accountability, greater responsibility and transparency through social audits and evaluations of institutions. Moreover, there is need to review the logic of project financing so private social investment initiatives can contribute to strengthening the non-profit sector and philanthropy. This includes contributing to the sustainability and strengthening of social organizations for the development and retention of human resources, and the training of media in social issues.

Challenges are many, but opportunities are also many. The e-Philanthropy is a good example of what can be done in the Internet to mobilize increased resources for social causes. There are several examples of how with a single click, you can mobilize resources without any effort.

The current context is also conducive to cooperative development, to work together. A good example to illustrate this is the Network America, where it is possible to establish cooperation with organizations from other countries and work together to define a regional position.

There are also excellent opportunities for the development of corporate social investment. The foundation is a very interesting model because it offers stability, maintenance and focus of action. On the other hand, foundations have very strict statutes. Companies are more flexible in their social investment and are therefore easier to support non-traditional models, as for example, micro finance and social entrepreneurship. There are also very simple things that the company can do, for example, the teaming method, which is to create micro-donations in team, so you can channel a lot of resources. The company only needs to coordinate the initiative.

Now it is time to further advance the social investment in Latin America, spreading values of citizenship and solidarity to an increasing group of people, the whole society, so it can take ownership of these goods, which are, after all, public property.

※

BRASIL
Fernando Rosetti,
General Secretariat, GIFE

The discussion about Social Investment in Latin America must answer questions regarding the definition of roles, the distinction between Private Social Investment (PSI) and Corporate Social Responsibility (CSR); consolidation of the PSI and funding the voluntary and non-profit Sector.

DEFINITION OF ROLES

There is still a serious difficulty in defining the roles of the three major sectors of society: government, business and voluntary sector. Despite dating back to the early 90's, the image below is still the current image of private social investment.

GIFE, 2007

The state has been weakened in the speeches of the 90's. It used to be said that the state was poorly managed and, therefore, companies and civil society should fulfil a larger role in building a sustainable society. In the 90's there were entrepreneurs who believed it was necessary to privatize the public education system.

Currently there is a more developed collective perception that it is impossible to think of social investment without thinking about the role of the state. Private social investment and civil society are organized in accordance or in interface with the public policies offered by the state. So we need to create possibilities to these three distinct actors – who have rhythm, culture, and different aspirations – to meet and formulate proposals for the public good, for what belongs to us all, but is not necessarily of the estate.

DISTINCTION BETWEEN PRIVATE SOCIAL INVESTMENT AND CORPORATE SOCIAL RESPONSIBILITY

Corporate Social Responsibility is business management in a sustainable and responsible way with all the different public related to the company. And private social investment is the voluntary contribution – this is perhaps the most important word, volunteer means that the company makes the contribution because it wants to, there is no legal obligation to do so – of private resources, here the term resources is to make it clear that it is not just about financial support, because the contribution can be competence, knowledge, materials. Private social investment differs from the welfare models of action in society because this investment of resources in society is planned, systematic, and monitored.

CORPORATE SOCIAL RESPONSABILITY	VS	PRIVATE SOCIAL INVESTMENT
It is the management way that is defined by ethics and transparent relation of the company with all the publics that it has relation with		It is the voluntary and systematic allocation of private resources in a planned and monitored way, to social projects with public interests
ETHO'S concept		GIFE'S concept

| PRIVATE RESOURCES TO PRIVATE PURPOSES | | PRIVATE RESOURCES TO PUBLIC PURPOSES |

GIFE, 2007

10 or 15 years ago in Brazil, corporate social responsibility and private social investment were in different fields. Corporate social responsibility was more in the field of private business management, of the company, while private social investment was more in the public arena, NGOs, the voluntary sector and of the state. What do we see from the year 2000? Companies are becoming increasingly social, and NGOs and all organizations of civil society becoming increasingly entrepreneurial. This is not only happening in Brazil, but worldwide, where there is no clear distinction between social and private, as it is sometimes difficult to determine if an action of a company is a private social investment or corporate social responsibility. This distinction is made more difficult by the "win-win" shares, where the community and the company earn.

Moreover, there is an interesting phenomenon going on: organizations that were designed to work with private social investment, are now called by companies to help facilitate the relationship with several of their stakeholders. In other words, a new role for corporate foundations is emerging. In this role the foundation not only works out with the community, but it brings to the company a social, environmental and cultural repertoire, and helps the company to build business plans that incorporate more sustainable relationships. This is a time of transition in which the definition of corporate social investment is impoverished by the complexity of actions that can be observed.

PSI CONSOLIDATION

From the classic definition of private social investment and the observation of the organizations working in private social investment, you can see a typology, as illustrated below.

GIFE, 2007.

The first type refers to welfare, charity: the donor deals with the symptom and not the cause of the social problem, which means it gives coats, food, campaigns on Christmas to donate toys, but the action is unsystematic and poorly planned.

A second model, which is very common in business organizations, may be called multi-project. It occurs when the organization begins to work with the school and realizes that the problem of the school involves the children's families, and then begins to work with the families, and then realizes that it is no good working with families if it does not work income generation, then begins to work in income generation, then realizes that they will have to make partnership, and does it, with the government. The result of these actions is a multi-project social work where there is no apparent alignment between the business and the social projects of the company. This does not stand for long time. Someone in the board will ask: why do we do all these things? What is the result of our work?

When the question is well designed, the organization starts searching for focus. What characterizes the search for focus is that the organization spends more energy within than outside. Even organizations that have their focus, have a mission, a vision and a strategy defined, after some time working they feel the need to expand the range of actions and have periodically to come back into focus.

Once focus, mission and vision are defined, then it is possible to define action, indicators and assessment strategies. Finally, the passage from the strategies to the field of social technologies and public policies is matter of scaling: how do I do it bigger? How do I deal with complex problems? And here, the only way, in fact, are cross sector partnerships.

FINANCING THE NOT-FOR-PROFIT SECTOR

Where did the money that created the voluntary and not-for-profit sector come from? This discussion on the funding of civil society organizations is important as a challenge to social investment, so that it can contribute to a sustainable society.

In the 90s, there was a very important international help to develop the voluntary sector in Brazil. GIFE, for example, took part at meetings in the American Chamber of Commerce, received very significant contributions from the Kellogg Foundation and has received significant money contributions from the Avina Foundation and the Ford Foundation for their development. Currently, Ford, Kellogg, Avina, Mott Foundation and Open Society, are the five foundations that finance the infrastructure of civil society in the world. However, international aid is changing its profile. The strategy for Brazil and Latin America is getting closer to a new approach of bringing knowledge, methodology and tools, but its funding is local and not international anymore. And some of the big foundations are shifting their focus to Africa and Asia.

Another area that traditionally invests in civil society is the government, either through outsourcing services that start being developed by civil society, or through fundraising for programs in partnership.

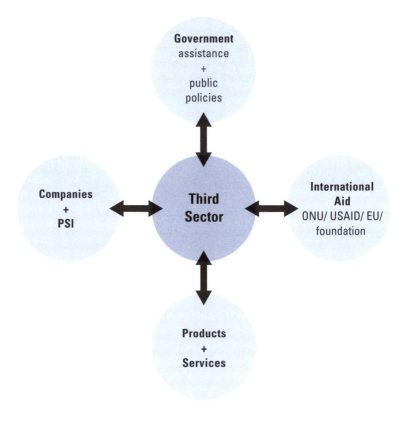

GIFE, 2007.

The data of money flow and resources available for the voluntary and not-for-profit sector are quite fragile, if not nonexistent. But we know that the number of non-profit foundations tripled in Brazil in the last 15 years. In 2007, there were 275 thousand foundations and non-profit organisations in the country. Consequently, competition for resources is much tougher.

The voluntary sector is becoming a market in which people compete for money. This is good because you are forced to become more professional. We also see the birth and survival of strong organizations, but local social organizations – grassroots organizations, small organizations working with neighbourhoods and communities – have an enormous difficulty of funding. And everybody who works in the social sector knows about the importance of these grassroots organizations. Now we face the challenge of identifying and supporting sustainability in the base of society, which meets local needs and press for more consistent public policies. This is a challenge for private social investment if we think like an agent that strengthens not only the state but also the basis of society, contributing to a more sustainable society.

SOCIAL INVESTMENT IN LATIN AMERICA:
LOOKING AT THE FUTURE

OPPORTUNITIES AND CHALLENGES[8]

Private social investment in Latin America is growing and strengthening: the amount of resources available for social investment is growing, both financial and human; there is greater awareness by both the company and civil society about the importance of private social investment; and there is greater public recognition of private social investment contribution for society. In almost every country of the continent there is an institution that professionally promotes social investment made by companies. Therefore, in the last ten years a significant asset of organizations devoted to social investment was built, such as GIFE and IDIS in Brazil, GDFE in Argentina and Cemefi in Mexico.

Moreover, the last ten years of private social investment practice and development in the region have contributed to acquired knowledge and the creation of learning and exchange networks, such as the Network America, the Company Forum and the Inter-American Network of Social Responsibility Research. Finally, we should also record the great interest and professionalism of the media on issues of private social investment.

---

8. In September 23rd, 2007, the workshop "Analyses of Social Investment in Latin America" lead by IDIS and facilitated by Fernando Rossetti, general secretary of GIFE, has put together 54 leaders of the sector to discuss the context of private social investment in Latin America. The chosen participants represent a vast variety of organizations such as private foundations, universities and associations. The discussion tackled four axes: strengthens, opportunities, weaknesses and threatens and it has raise valuable input to think the future of private social investment in the region.

In this context of growth and vigour, it is possible to identify many opportunities to develop and further strengthen private social investment in the region. Among them are:

OPPORTUNITIES

Mobilizing people and resources: the current (and growing) awareness of society about social issues and equity represents an excellent time to mobilize more people and resources for private social investment, not only with regard to corporate social investment but also the possibility of increasing the interest of families, individuals and communities in private social investment, thereby creating opportunities for expansion of family social investment and community social investment.

Innovation in private social investment: If on one hand the society, aware of social issues, demonstrates higher expectations about the effectiveness and results of social investment, on the other it is more open to new ways of acting. There is then the opportunity to develop new forms of social investment, experimenting with hybrid models that mix social sector approaches and private sector practices, such as social entrepreneurship and venture philanthropy.

Economic Globalization: The globalization of the economy in Latin America has contributed to the rapid growth of corporate social investment in the region, leading multinationals and local companies to increasingly act in private social investment. Moreover, the growing influence of the movement of corporate social responsibility contributes to a better understanding of systemic thinking and the interrelationship between economic, social and environmental factors for a sustainable development.

Production of Knowledge: Finally, we highlight the opportunity to develop the area of knowledge production, research, and professionalization of people working in the social sector. Unfolding new experiences and learning, grows the need to systematize and disseminate this knowledge.

Although many successes and results have been achieved over the last fifteen years of private social investment in Latin America, there are also a number of weaknesses that require consideration and action. The sector remains with a tendency to institutional corporatism, that is, follow the specific interests of the institution of private social investment rather than support the community's social development priorities. It is when the agenda of private investment is placed above the social and the goals and policies of private institutions with social arms is more aligned to the interests of the company that to issues and social priorities of the country. In this situation there is no clear understanding of whether it is or not possible and favourable to work in network and alliance, in common causes aligned to national priorities.

Another weak aspect of private social investment in the region which needs to be strengthened concerns the question of scalability. Many third-sector projects have got quality, but can not impact in scale. Quality, quantity and low cost is a common challenge for private social investment in Latin America. For example, in Brazil, the public sector, in either health or education, is able to meet the demand of quantity: currently, 97% of Brazilian children are in school. However, the quality is very low. When the not-for-profit sector conducts successful actions and effective results, the quality increases, but the quantity is reduced. So the challenge of scalability is the performance with quantity, quality and low cost. Evaluation of measurable results and clear benchmarks, comparable indicators and national results are needed for scalability. It is also necessary to strengthen areas of cooperation and conciliation, to become more efficient rather than just a place where good intentions are discussed but never implemented into action.

Training and qualification of leadership is also weak. The current qualification and professionalization of the not-for-profit sector leaders does not meet the high heterogeneity among the wide and varied range of organizations that make up the sector. It results in great difficulty and delay in the interaction among the various actors, because there are different degrees of understanding and training. Moreover, there is a growing need to understand this new area of expertise offered by private social investment which encompasses social, financial and administrative constraints that demand new logic and new practices.

Another aspect that needs to be tackled is concerning the governance of private social investment. As many are family companies, several institutes and corporate foundations have mixed boards, which are composed of both representatives of the family and representatives of the company. This often causes deadlocks and lack of leadership. The governance model needs to be strengthened, so that it not only addresses the interests of the council, but also of the beneficiaries of social investment.

Finally, we must think private social investment sustainably. In this sense, it is worrying the discontinuity of social projects and programs, and the "systemic amnesia" of certain organizations that often change their whole team and start again from scratch, without continuing previous initiatives. There is also a large gap between the pace of corporate social investment decisions and the pace of social organizations, i.e. the executors of social investment.

Besides knowing the weaknesses and shortcomings of the sector that need to be addressed and strengthened; it is also important to understand that there are external environment challenges in which private social investment must be prepared to act.

CHALLENGES

Strengthening of public and legal sector: Political instability of governments, the inefficiency of public administration and weaknesses of the regulatory framework are challenges still present in Latin America. The populist governments are also a challenge because for them perpetuating poverty and low levels of education might be convenient.

Awareness: The lack of culture and knowledge of social investment by some private companies may also be considered a challenge for the industry. There are some private companies that still maintain a welfare approach and working in a reactive way, when in reality, it is necessary to generate proactive actions. Another challenge is to promote business leaders' participation and qualification on private social investment issues.

Transparency in the not-for-profit sector: The sector represents a wide range of organizations and is often seen by society as a point of corruption. In some countries of the region there is a lot of resistance and distrust in the voluntary sector and in social organizations. It is therefore essential to develop mechanisms of transparency, accountability, and classification of social organizations to strengthen the sector's credibility.

The following table summarizes the strengths and weaknesses, as well as the opportunities and challenges of private social investment in Latin America.

STRENGTHS	WEAKNESSES
• Availability of human and financial resources • Society Awareness • Public recognition • Accumulated Knowledge • Professional organizations dedicated to the PSI (IDIS, Cemefi, GDFE, GIFE) • Learning and exchange Networks (Network America, Business Forum) • Media Interest	• Institutional Corporatism • Lack of cooperation culture • Scalability • Evaluation • Sustainability • Qualified Leadership • Governance

OPPORTUNITIES	CHALLENGES

• Mobilization of more people and resources
• Globalization of the economy: increased access to global business
• Innovation:
  • Social entrepreneurship
  • Venture Philanthropy
  • Community Foundations
  • Family Foundations
• Knowledge production
• Education, training and qualification of human resources
• Information technology
	• Strengthening of public sector
	• Regulatory framework
	• Political stability
	• Populist Governments
	• Awareness
	• Transparency in the not-for-profit sector

THE COMPANY AND THE FAMILY AS SOCIAL INVESTORS: CHARACTERISTICS, CHALLENGES AND THEIR RELATIONSHIP WITH CIVIL SOCIETY AND THE PUBLIC SECTOR

Regardless of who is the private social investor, whether business, family or community, the intention is common to all: make resources (human, financial, material, and technical, etc.) available for the public good, in order to generate positive social impact. However, as social investor, each of these actors has specific values and logic. While the corporate social investment tends to be the expression of the ethos of the company, family social investment can be used to teach the next generation the value of money. While family social investment has got the flexibility to choose its focus, corporate social investment demand is aligned with the business and corporate strategy. While families tend to worry about long-term performance, with perpetuity, corporate executives tend to have a more immediate, short-term, social investment.

CORPORATE SOCIAL INVESTMENT

The company's main purpose is to produce goods and services, generate jobs and distribute dividends to shareholders and investors. But besides being an economic entity, the company presents itself in society as an ethic and social entity, since it uses resources and takes up space that are property of the whole society.

In recent decades, we had a larger business involvement with local communities' social issues. It is increasingly more difficult to isolate the company's business without considering its socio-environmental impact because society asks for a growing socially responsible and sustainable business. Its voluntary participation in the community, if properly planned, monitored and evaluated, can contribute to cause major social changes, generating benefits for the community and the company.

When a company decides to have its social arm, it is essential to define the focus of its social investment. This definition, however, tends to be a provocative process as the social investment program is bound to a target audience, typically the public where the company operates, but not necessarily the target audience of the business.

Usually there is a dynamic relationship between the two parts, in which the growth of the social arm of the company follows the growth of the business. Thus, companies' foundations and institutes change and evolve as the dynamism of the company's stock. Moreover, as the purpose of foundations and institutes is public, they have the power to lead and influence the company to also recognize its purpose in society. To promote this relationship between the company and its social arm it is essential to integrate, via corporate volunteers, the employees of the company with its social performance. Thus, company and foundation are complementary.

It is worth noting an important difference in social investment among family-controlled companies and joint stock companies. In the case of family-controlled companies, conviction and engagement with stakeholders facilitate the integrated management and change process can be accelerated in comparison to joint stock companies.

In short, dynamic and close relationship between the company and its social arm is crucial. This requires engaging employees in the social arm of the company to overcome internal competition and overlap of activities between the two, clearly defining the roles of business and foundation/institute.

FAMILY SOCIAL INVESTMENT

Family originated foundations are free to choose the focus of their activities. However, the challenge for family foundations is to choose a focus that expresses the family values and represents the interests of the family activities. Another major challenge is to ensure the involvement of future generations in social investment.

The issue of governance is very important, especially with regard to transparency and definition of roles and responsibilities. Usually there is an advisory council composed of family members and executive oversight to implement the decisions. The presence of family members on the board can create tensions; therefore each one should have a very clear role. While it is the board's role to establish guidelines and make strategic decisions, it is not its role to deal with operational details. Therefore, family members must understand that they need to stay away from the operation of the foundation.

Traditionally, family foundations work in isolation and independently, based on their own practice. However, there is now a growing trend of openness and collaboration, conducting work in partnerships or alliances, sharing experiences and supporting projects of other organizations.

Finally, in contemplating corporate and family social investments, it is worth exploring the possibilities of cooperation and collaboration between the two. Is it possible to reconcile the interests of family shareholders, with the interests of the company? Are the values of family and business complementary? Can they relate? What is the role of the family manager?

The controlling shareholder can help to enhance the relationship foundation – company, representing both the interests of the family and the company and also bringing a long-term and sustainable vision not always common to executives. It can also support the foundation in its role as provoking, from family values, new issues in the company. Reconciling the social vision of the foundation with the business vision of the corporation is not an easy task. The clearer the focus that unites the company and the foundation more sustainable their relationship will be.

Finally, a crucial issue that permeates both the world of foundations as well as the world of family businesses is leadership succession. Both organizations need to be alert to this issue and conduct continuous activities to support the training of leaders, working with several generations of the family.

SOCIAL INVESTOR RELATIONSHIP WITH THE PUBLIC SECTOR: COLLABORATION OR REPLACEMENT?

Private social investment can – and should – help shaping public policy. Even with the diversity found in Latin America and the rise of populist policies, there is still much room for working in partnership with governments in the region. As the end of private investment is the public benefit, it is inevitable the relationship with the government.

Public Policy includes government decisions in several areas that influence the lives of a group of citizens. These are the acts that the government does or does not do and the effects that such actions or absence of these causes in society. The social investor can contribute so that existing policies effectively reach those most in need, for example, promoting the adoption of models of public management, or influencing the prioritization of resources to specific areas or programs.

The awareness of co-responsibility for development has led to an increasing number of public policies based on successful experiences of social organizations, enterprises, institutes and private foundations. When a project becomes public policy, it wins greater coverage, and apart of benefiting more people, it helps disseminating successful actions.

In this alliance between the public sector and the private social investor there are three issues that often present less difficulties in regard to partnerships: education, frequent theme in all countries of the region; income generation and community development.

Working with local governments is very important, in that way both government and private investors are more likely to assess the impact of social actions. The partnership with local government involves issues such as political wills, ethic commitment, technical competence and trust. It is one of the roles of social investors to adapt to the bureaucracy and to the government's rigid hierarchy, without giving in to welfare, unfortunately still common in many government programs.

Although it is important and desirable to influence in public policy, it is not the only way to work private social investment and not all opportunities have to be taken. It depends on the moment, on the capabilities of the investor and on convenience.

Finally, the private social investment has an important role in supporting and promoting the participation of the community, and more than directly influencing public policies, the investor should through his programs create capacity in communities so that they may influence public policy.

SOCIAL INVESTOR RELATIONSHIP WITH CIVIL SOCIETY: DONATION OR PARTNERSHIP?

It is desirable that the relationship between social organizations and the organizations become more horizontal: that social investor is not seen only as a donor, a provider of resources, but really as a partner or associate. On the other hand, it is important to recognize the capacity, autonomy and knowledge of social organizations.

There are different ways to make organizations co-responsible for the projects. The funding of projects can, for example, apply criteria of performance, effectiveness and results. Another approach is to work with a cofinancing, where social organizations contribute with their assets, not necessarily economic resources, but time, volunteers, facilities, etc.

It is not possible to have a good impact if there is no relationship between government, business and civil society. Therefore, communication between sectors, identifying the projects that each one is doing is essential to the sustainability of development processes. It is very important to have a communication policy within and between organizations so their objectives are known. Thus, it increases transparency and functions as a mechanism to identify synergies and avoid suspicion.

The concept of sustainability encompasses many aspects. It is not only understood as a project that is renewed, but also as the generation of knowledge. It also includes sustainability in the management of organizations, so they are able to create other projects. Development is a process of cooperation and the strengthening of the entities institutional process is essential.

It is crucial that investors know and understand the needs of the community. Therefore, it is important that corporate foundations know the community and develop a relationship of trust. The first approximation of the social investor with the community is the most important. The community's assets, knowledge and needs must be identified. Often, this approach can be done through community leaders or through other organizations already working in the same community, even if not with the same issues. In this scenario, participatory methods tend to generate positive results.

To be participatory is necessary that the process is plural, involving diverse groups, with different thoughts. In selecting projects, for example, it is essential for the call to be transparent and plural. Often the process of beneficiary selection leaves out small, creative organizations that work closely with the community because the call process is very complex. For example, a call can not be only via electronic means, but other forms of communication such as posters or word of mouth by community leaders must also be used. This is important not to banish in the call process the possibility of meeting small organizations that work close to the community and have valuable knowledge.

The social investor must be focused enough and flexible enough to be able to act on the causes of problems and not only in its effects. One should always think in a more systemic way, without losing focus. The causes of the problems, on the other hand, are variable and, therefore, the social investor must also be flexible in the process of selecting beneficiaries. He must learn to identify the variables that cause the problems.

The social investor seeks to support innovative projects. However, there is always more risk with innovative projects but because they are innovative, they can bring a higher return. It is therefore important that social investment have also tolerance to failure, because much can be learnt with it. Finally, the social investor must be aware that there is a risk of failure and that much can be learned from that. After all, the failure may be the key to future success.

CONCLUSION

Private social investment is an efficient mean to promote social development, re-distribute private wealth and create ways of working to boost the balance and harmonious development of society.

In Latin America, shortcomings in large social groups are still found: poverty, marginalization and inequality persist and grow. The solution of these problems is the responsibility of the whole society. In recent decades groups of citizens have become more aware of their social responsibility and are organized as voluntary associations to participate in the search for alternatives and projects designed for community well being. Also, more and more companies are increasing their participation in social development, contributing with talent and resources.

Philanthropy appears in all the world's great religions and civilizations: Christianity, Islam, and Buddhism; Asia, Africa and Latin America. There were philanthropists between capitalists and socialists, as well as among missionaries of different faiths. Philanthropy is also present in the acts of the government and for many years the question of how much people should do on their own, how much should be done by volunteers and how much the state should do.

The principles of the new philanthropy or private social investment, discussed in this forum, show that we should not act emotionally and impulsively, but based on evidence, on careful analysis and planning. It is always preferable to prevent social problems to deal with them later on.

As discussed there are several challenges for private social investment in Latin America. According to the World Wealth Report 2007, a study of the wealthiest investors in the world conducted by Capgemini and Merrill Lynch, the richest people in the region commit only 3% of their assets to charitable donations. In comparison, the Asian tycoons donate 12% of their money, in the Middle East 8%, Americans 8% and Europeans 5%.

Our continent is also rich in creativity and innovation. Social Investment needs to be fed by the energy that we recognize in each of the countries of Latin America. During the days of the Forum, we were able to reflect on the world of social investment, which was the goal of this meeting. In a way, each participant is a protagonist of the story that is told here and participates in the future, in the story that was written there and from this meeting. We know that we could not bring up any issues that may worry us in the field of social investment and we are certain that not all questions were answered. But what was seen here can be the agenda for future actions.

We know where we came from and we have a direction of the future, but we do not know yet what we will find later because there are variables, risks that are not under our control. As Guimarães Rosa said, "Living, we learn, but what you learn more, is to make other major questions." So, we leave with more concerns and questions to be answered. To continue, we have to exercise a strategic capacity, interpreting reality to find opportunities to be stronger, to avoid the dangers and transform weaknesses into strengths.

ANNEXES

ANNEX A: PARTICIPANT LIST

Alejandro Martinez, Fundación Merced
Alicia Pimentel, Fundación Empresas Polar
Ana Beatriz B. Patrício, Fundação Itaú Social
Ana Maria Drummond, Instituto WCF-Brasil
Ana Petrini, Fundación Minetti
Ana Valéria Nascimento Araújo Leitão, Fundo Brasil de Direitos Humanos
Beatriz Johanpeter, Instituto Gerdau
Carla Duprat, Grupo Camargo Corrêa
Carlos March, Fundación Avina
Carolina Langan, Grupo de Fundaciones y Empresas
Célia Schlithler, IDIS
Celso Varga, IDIS
Ceres Loise Bertelli Gabardo, Fundação O Boticário de Proteção à Natureza
Claiton Melo, Fundação Banco do Brasil
Claudio Giomi, Fundación Arcor
Consuelo Yoshida, IDIS
Corina Ferrer Minetti de Lozada, Fundación Minetti
Cristina Galindez Hernandez, The William and Flora Hewlett Foundation – Mexico
Dario Guarita Neto, Fundação Maria Cecilia Souto Vidigal
Eduardo Valente, Instituto Vivo
Elizabeth Kfuri Simão, Grupo Coimex
Enrique Morad, Fundación Loma Negra
Fernando Nogueira, GIFE
Fernando Rossetti, GIFE
Flavio Martín Flores Acevedo, Asociación Los Andes de Cajamarca
Graciela Pantin, Fundación Empresas Polar
Guillermo Carvajalino, Fundación Empresarios por la Educación

Gustavo Lara Alcántara, Fundación BBVA Bancomer
Helena Monteiro, IDIS
Jorge V. Villalobos Grzybowicz, CEMEFI
José Eduardo Sabo Paes, Promotoria de Justiça e Fundações e Entidades de Interesse Social

Juan Andrés Garcia, Associacíon Española de Fundaciones
Juliana Gazzotti Schneider, IDIS
Manuel José Carvajal, Fundación Carvajal
Márcia Woods, IDIS
Marcos Kisil, IDIS
Margareth Dicker Goldenberg, Instituto Ayrton Senna
Michael Liffman, Asia-Pacific Centre for Philanthropy and Social Investment Swinburne University
Miguel Gaitán, Fundación Pantaleon
Olavo Gruber Neto, Fundação Orsa
Olívia Tanahara, Fundação Orsa
Regina Vidigal Guarita, Fundação Maria Cecilia Souto Vidigal
Rob Buchanan, Council on Foundation
Roberto Pizzarro, Fundación Carvajal
Rodrigo Villar Gómez, Fundación DIS
Rosangela Bacima, Instituto Pão de Açúcar
Russell Prior, CAF
Scot Marken, Donors Forum of South Florida
Sérgio Amoroso, Fundação Orsa
Sérgio Mindlin, Fundação Telefônica
Silvia Bertoncini, IDIS
Silvia Morais, Instituto Hedging-Griffo
Susan Saxon-Harrold, CAF America
Wilberto Luiz Lima Junior, Klabin

ANNEX B:
SPEAKERS AND AUTHOR'S
MINI-BIOGRAPHIES

Carolina Langan has a degree in Sociology from the Universidad de Buenos Aires with a Masters in Administration and Public Policy at the Universidad de San Andrés. She was the general coordinator and executive director of the civil association "Puentes" in 1998. Currently she is the general coordinator of the Grupo de Fundaciones y Empresas (GDFE). Author of the publication "Studies of social investment: an approach to the study of grant making foundations in Argentina" and co-author of "Social investment guide." Specialist in the design and evaluation of programs and social projects and topics related to private social investment.

Fernando Rossetti is general secretary of GIFE (Grupo de Institutos, Fundações e Empresas) and chairman of Wings (Worldwide Initiatives for Grantmakers Support). He graduated in Social Sciences at Unicamp, worked in the newspaper Folha de S. Paulo from 1990 to 1999 as an education reporter and as correspondent in South Africa (1994-95). He is specialized in Human Rights from Columbia University (USA, 1997). With Gilberto Dimenstein founded, the NGO Cidade Escola Aprendiz that he directed from 1999 to 2002. He acted as consultant to several national and international organizations of the voluntary sector, such as UNICEF, for whom he wrote the book "Media and School – Perspectives for public policy." He is a commentator at Canal Futura since 1997, Synergos Senior Fellow and leader-partner Avina.

Jorge Villalobos Grzybowicz is the president of the Mexican Centre for Philanthropy, Cemefi, founded in 1988 with the mission to promote the culture of philanthropy and social responsibility. He has got a wide experience in development projects and social advancements for civil society organizations. He was the coordinator of the Communication College at the Universidade Ibero-americana. Since 1990 collaborates with the Mexican Centre for Philanthropy. He is part of the citizen council for social development of the Development and Technical Advisory Council on Social Development as well as of several other boards of foundations and associations.

Juan Andres Garcia holds a degree in Geography and History from the Universidad Complutense of Madrid. He was the director of the Foundations Centre, director of the Spanish Association of Foundations. Participated in the organization and dissemination of the Ibero-American Meeting of the Third Sector and is a board member of the AEF. He is a patron of two Spanish foundations for social purposes. He has collaborated with several books and publications such as the "Directory of Spanish Foundations" and "La responsabilidad de la Global Wealth".

Marcos Kisil is CEO of IDIS and a Professor at the University of São Paulo, School of Public Health. Prior to this position, he was regional director for Latin America and the Caribbean of the W. K. Kellogg Foundation, where he directed the strategic and programmatic development of activities in Latin America. Marcos Kisil is graduated at the faculty of medicine of the University of Sao Paulo. Later, he acted in the field of health administration, and received a doctorate degree in administration from George Washington University, Washington, USA and a fellow of the WK Kellogg Foundation. He worked as consultant for the Pan American Health Organization. He is senior fellow of Synergos and is a member of the boards of Resource Alliance and Save Brasil – BirdLive International.

Michael Liffman is founding director of the Asia-Pacific Centre for Philanthropy and Social Investment at Swinburne University, Melbourne, Australia. The centre offers vocational and academic education in social investment, in addition to doing research and consultancy in Australia and other countries. Michael has experience in social public policy, community service and social investment. He was president of one of Australia's leading foundations, the Myers Foundation, and president of the Australian Association of Philanthropy. He was a member of the International Network on Strategic Philanthropy. His publications include "A Tradition of Giving: Seventy-five Years of Myer Family Philanthropy," (Melbourne University Publishing, 2004). He has got a Master's degree in Social Administration from the London School of Economics and a PhD.

Rob Buchanan is director of international programs of the Council on Foundations in Washington, USA. The Council on Foundations is an association of public interest by promoting social investment in the United States and the world. Rob has worked for ten years at Oxfam America and also in EarthAction. He served as adviser to the U.S. Senate and the House of Representatives in international politics. Rob is a graduate of The Johns Hopkins University and has got a master's degree in international relations from The Johns Hopkins School of Advanced International Studies. He is co-author of "Making a Difference in Africa: Advice from Experienced Grant makers" published in 2004. Rob is currently a board member of the Asia Pacific Philanthropy Consortium.

Russell Prior is Head of Enterprise and Philanthropy Development at the Charities Aid Foundation. Russell is responsible for CAF's client relationship management, business development, sales and distribution, advisory and consulting services, product management and international network. Before joining CAF in 2005 Russell was with Barclays where he gained a wealth of specialist knowledge and experience of banking and finance, both in the UK and internationally. Russell was Chair of the National Finance Hub and is a trustee of a number of Foundations focused on supporting development in the fast growing economies. He serves on the Governing Council of the European Foundation Centre.

Scott Marken is president and CEO of the Donors Forum of South Florida since 2004. Donors Forum of South Florida is an association of foundations, corporations, individuals and government active funds in Miami, Ft Lauderdale, Palm Beach and Florida Keys. The members of the Donors Forum have contributed more than $600 million per year in one of the most multi-cultural regions of the United States. Previously, Marken was CEO of an international consultancy working on social investment with customers like Ericsson, Burger King and Rotary International.

AUTHORS

Helena Monteiro is Director of Knowledge and Education of IDIS. Prior to this position, Helena accumulated over 15 years experience in the social sector in Canada and the USA, dedicated to projects in education, health and social development. She has also worked in international cooperation, coordinating projects in education and health of the Pan American Health Organization (PAHO), the Organization of American States (OAS) and the Canadian Association of Public Health. Helena is an educator licensed by the Catholic University of São Paulo – PUC, Master of Social Work by the University of Toronto, Canada, and Senior Fellow at the Centre on Philanthropy and Civil Society, City University of New York (CUNY), USA.

Márcia Kalvon Woods works in IDIS since 2002 and as the Director of Institutional Development in IDIS, since 2007. Widely experienced in fundraising, marketing for non-profit organizations and cause related marketing. Previously, she worked in the marketing area of the Australian Red Cross, Shaklee Corporation, and 3M do Brasil. With a degree in Social Communication from ESPM – Escola Superior de Propaganda e Marketing (College of Advertising and Marketing), she took extension courses at the University of São Paulo – USP/IDIS, at FGV – Fundação Getúlio Vargas, and at the University of California.

Marcos Kisil is CEO of IDIS and a Professor at the University of São Paulo, School of Public Health. Prior to this position, he was regional director for Latin America and the Caribbean of the W. K. Kellogg Foundation, where he directed the strategic and programmatic development of activities in Latin America. Marcos Kisil is graduated at the faculty of medicine of the University of Sao Paulo. Later, he acted in the field of health administration, and received a doctorate degree in administration from George Washington University, Washington, USA and a fellow of the WK Kellogg Foundation. He worked as consultant for the Pan American Health Organization. He is senior fellow of Synergos and is a member of the boards of Resource Alliance and Save Brasil – BirdLive International.

PRIVATE SOCIAL INVESTMENT TRENDS IN LATIN AMERICA

	INSTITUTO PARA O DESENVOLVIMENTO DO INVESTIMENTO SOCIAL
Writers:	Helena Monteiro, Márcia Kalvon Woods, Marcos Kisil
Coordination:	Márcia Kalvon Woods
Translator:	Paula Sporleder

imprensaoficial	**IMPRENSA OFICIAL DO ESTADO DE SÃO PAULO**
Graphic Design and Cover:	Guen Yokoyama
Editorial Assistant:	Berenice Abramo
Publishing:	Marilena Villavoy
Graphics:	Robson Minghini

Sponsorship:	CAF, Fundação Vale do Rio Doce, Fundação Banco do Brasil, Gerdau, Instituto Camargo Corrêa y Fundación Loma Negra

Copyright © 2011 by IDIS – Institute for the Development of Social Investment

Catalog-in-Publication (CIP)
(Câmara Brasileira do Livro, SP, Brazil)

Private Social Investment Tendencies in Latin America / organizers Helena Monteiro, Marcos Kisil, Márcia Woods – 1st ed. – São Paulo: IDIS – Instituto para o Desenvolvimento do Investimento Social: Imprensa Oficial do Estado de São Paulo, 2011.
84 p.

Several authors

ISBN 978-85-60904-09-9 (IDIS)
ISBN 978-85-7060-993-9 (Imprensa Oficial)

1. Social Action – Latin America 2. Companies – Social Aspects – Latin America 3. Social Participation I. Monteiro, Helena. II. Kisil, Marcos. III. Woods, Márcia.

09-12708   CDD 361.760981

Systematical Catalog Indexes
1. Latin America: Social Investment:
   Private Organizations: Social Welfare
   361.760981
2. Latin America: Private Organizations:
   Social Investment: Social Welfare
   361.760981

The whole or partial reproduction
without publisher's prior permission
is not allowed

Rights reserved and protected
(Lei nº 9.610, de 19.02.1998)

The legal filing was made at Biblioteca Nacional
(Lei nº 10.994, de 14.12.2004)

Printed in Brazil 2011

Instituto para o Desenvolvimento do Investimento Social
Rua Paes Leme, 524, cj. 141
Pinheiros 05424 904
São Paulo SP Brasil
Tel.: 11 3037 8210
Fax: 11 3031 9052
www.idis.org.br

CAF – Charities Aid Foundation
25 Kings Hill Avenue
Kings Hill
West Malling
Kent ME19 4TA UK
T: +44 0 3000 123 000
F: +44 0 3000 123 001
enquiries@cafonline.org
www.cafonline.org

Imprensa Oficial do Estado de São Paulo
Rua da Mooca, 1.921 Mooca
03103 902 São Paulo SP Brasil
sac 0800 01234 01
sac@imprensaoficial.com.br
livros@imprensaoficial.com.br
www.imprensaoficial.com.br

Format	15,5 x 23 cm
Typology	Chaparral Pro and ITC Franklin Gothic Std
Papers	miolo Offset 90 g/m^2
	cover Supreme Card Duo Design 300 g/m^2
Pages	84
Draught	1.200 copies
CTP, Printing and Finishing	Imprensa Oficial do Estado de São Paulo

imprensaoficial